FORTY DAYS
AT THE CROSS

FORTY DAYS
AT THE CROSS

Arthur Blessitt

LAKELAND
BLUNDELL HOUSE
GOODWOOD ROAD
LONDON SE14 6BL

© Broadman Press 1971

Published in the United States of America by Broadman Press

First British Edition 1971

ISBN 0 551 00276 X

Typesetting by Witney Press, Witney, made and printed by Cox & Wyman Ltd., London, Reading and Fakenham

1ST DAY PRAYER

"Men ought always to pray and not to faint" (Luke 18: 1).

There is more pleasure in walking with Jesus one hour than in all the carnal pleasures of a lifetime!

When men are weak
            they *we*
                fail to pray.
The man, he cannot stand.
        Then But
            Jesus' hand reaches down
            to
            lift—
to hold.
to care.
to fill.

        Prayer
the beauty of
    our soul
                communication
                with the
Infinite Love,
            Truth
            And
                Sources of Life.
(A small candle can be seen from far away in darkness.)

True Prayer is getting *being* honest to God, yourself, your fellow man. *and woman*

How bright is your light to show the way?

Prayer is getting and giving,
          hearing and telling,
          going and doing.

Today I prayed all day. Twenty-four hours with Jesus—the
Bible—and friends.
Peace, victory, love, and power are what we desperately
need—in this hour with Him it's all here.
I saw some people cry—die to themselves—now to live in
joy and purpose.

          Before you start—pray.
          While you do it—pray.
          Before you stop—pray.

*"Lord, we faint without Thee, but with You we overcome;
take away our fear, fill us with faith. Thank You for the
victory. I praise Your name."*

2ND DAY
A LITTLE RAIN

"And let him that is athirst come. And whosoever will, let him take the water of life freely" (Rev. 22: 17).

"And the flood was forty days upon the earth; and the waters increased, and bare up the ark, and it was lift up above the earth" (Gen. 7: 17).

Water falls from
            up above—
Love's from up there,
                    too.
So let the love from
            up above
Flood me with love
            as fresh
As heaven's clear skies.

Rain drops
    give a little
        hope to troubled souls.

One day I sat in the rain and felt the wet, cool water drip from my cheek and blur my eyes. I saw creation lift up its arms to be filled. Dry crusty earth drank its fill and overflowed. Birds sang and frogs came out and the grass looked greener than before. Heavy clouds hung overhead and God's flashlight swept across the sky with a crack and boom. Water to give life to all, water to cool, water to keep things going, water to quench our thirst. Yes, I love the rain. I feel the fresh wind of new birth.

What a day! When God's heavenly rain washes away the pollution of hate, sin, hurt and
When the water of life fills our thirsty soul and lights the way to true life.

"Lord, just to let You fill me up, to overflow my soul with Your heavenly Love. Just put a drop of You within my soul. I'll never thirst again."

3RD DAY
THE POOR

"Blessed are the poor in spirit" (Matt. 5: 3).

"A little that a righteous man hath is better than the riches of many wicked" (Ps. 37: 16).

"Whoso hath this world's good, and seeth his brother have need and shutteth up his bowels of compassion from him, how dwelleth the love of God in him?" (1 John 3: 17).

"I don't think too much about the poor," a man said to me one day. "But the poor do," I replied.

How many will give themselves to the poor
   or
Spend time with the lonely, or hold the hand of a stranger?

   Have you ever seen
The poor trouble the conscience of the rich—Sometimes!

   Hear the cry of the poor.
Desperation in the face
                    of
                    the
                    child
Cold hands—
Bare feet—
No one caring where I sleep
                    who
                    will hear them crying?

Who will move from their bed's ease—
                    who
                    cares—who cares?

Poor
  but humble—
    proud—
Coins
  not
    bills
But—
  honest—
Not
  sold out for green leaves—
Poor—
  but free—
Hours
  are long—
But
  rest is sweet
Poor—
  but we still mean what we say.

The road is straight
  there's still
    black and white—
Remember there is no shame
    in poverty!

"Father, You love all, may we care as You, may the abundance of all You created be shared with every living soul in Jesus' name. Amen.

4TH DAY
THE ANSWER

"I am the way, the truth and the life; no man cometh unto the Father, but by me" (John 14: 6).

The answer is embodied in a person
                    Jesus Christ!

There is a way that
                    men do
                        try—
Somehow to find the way:
        We look
        We search
        We want to find—
        But
        for
        most we
                wait
                too
                late.

Have you ever looked for the Answer—then found it!
Life is kinda that way. Tragedy is—many never find life's greatest answer. Who am I—Why am I here—What do I live for—Where is eternity?
These questions probe—deep within—a million other questions spring forth. But there is hope!

The answer is not man's laws—but God's Love—
        only God can give real brotherhood.

Troops can't bring peace to the streets, homes or
troubled Land—
      but a new birth
           can.
The problem's not drugs, guns or crime—
                 the problem is people—
                 and
                 people problems—need
                 God's solution!

The Answer is simpler than the question!

*"O God, to know You, is life's answer, for in You all my
needs are met, and all of my brothers in the world can
walk together. Your trip is eternity, thanks for tuning me
in and for sending the Answer in the flesh."*

5TH DAY
REST

"Rest in the Lord" (Ps. 37: 7).

"Come unto me, all ye that labour and are heavy laden,
and I will give you rest. Take my yoke upon you, and
learn of me; for I am meek and lowly in heart: and ye
shall find rest unto your souls. For my yoke is easy, and
my burden is light" (Matt. 11: 28–30).

I'd like to rest a moment
        Stop—
           for just a
           while
And lie at rest . . .
Nothing to agitate my mind
        no
        pressure to perform
    Just lie at rest . . . for a long, long while.

  Have you ever lain in the clover, stretched on soft, warm,
green
And watched the clouds move slowly by as you felt the
evening Sun?
  Have you ever stood beside the sea, feet wet from
splashing waves upon
The soft, cool, crystal sand, and held up your hands as you
felt the mist in
  Your face?
  Have you ever sat for a long, long time and looked into
the eyes
Of the one you love, hands clasped in soft embrace and

knew that you were loved?

Rest, sweet Rest
Peace and Bliss,
Resting in
His Arms.

For what price can I buy rest?

Is rest an experience or condition?

Being a true Christian is not
constantly fighting but
Resting in the Lord.

Rest is painless—
even in pain.

You can rest—even while you cry.

Don't equate rest—with doing nothing.

People at rest can be most active.

Don't stop to rest—learn to rest all the time.

*"Lord, there are so many that need rest, send me to share
Thy peace, to those sick, lonely, and in need. May I share
all I have from Thee with my fellow man and may I rest
in Thee."*

6TH DAY
A SMILE

   —Smile
    God loves you!

I saw the sun smile
            and
            the
            clouds.
I saw the rainbow
          smile
            down
          at me.
And I laughed—a while.

I saw a mother smile
               and
               the infant
                    too
I stayed around a while—
             and
             smiled—
             a smile is like
                 a
             honey drop—
             a smile is like
             dew—
           a smile is a bit
                   of
               heaven
               when
          I hear you say, "I love you."

I like to smile; as a matter of fact
  I can't keep from it.

The smile of peace from a long heart-broken life is a true
delight.
To know that all is well—"whatever the Hell"—is really
where it's at!

A young hate-filled fellow stood facing me, a broken bottle
in his hand. "I'm going to kill you," he screamed. I stuck
out my hand to him, smiled, and said, "Brother, I love
you." I knelt to pray—after kicking me, he sat down beside
me, tears flowing down his cheek. "Arthur," he said, "I
know you love me. I need help!" He smiled as he knelt
down to pray.

"When God made everything" (He smiled)!

Take a little time to
                say
                hello
       Somebody needs
                your
                smile!

*"Lord, I'm glad You smiled down on me, put Your arm
around me and said, "Arthur, it's now O.K., I love to run
with you. Laugh, smile, and have fun with my heavenly
Daddy!"*

7TH DAY
VISION

"Where there is no vision, the people perish" (Prov. 29: 18).

"And that, knowing the time, that now it is high time to awake out of sleep" (Rom. 13: 11).

"Delight thyself in the Lord; and he shall give thee the desires of thine heart" (Ps. 37: 4).

If
only eyes could
            see
and
ears could
            hear

and
feelings
            feel.
If
only we could see
            beyond
            yonder
                hill
and
   care for
      another's
         ill.
if
only
   minds could

17

see
the
way it
could be—
Then
maybe
we could become
the person
we
should be.
but
most minds
are
closed within—
dreams
are
carnal—
Ideals—passed by
Energies
misplaced
but
God never gives dreams
that can't be
Realities.
So dream man
Let your mind soar
See visions—press on and
overcome.
Let the dreams move you,
keep seeing visions,
for
when visions end
and

```
          dreams cease
          you are dead; even
          before
                    you die!
```
Not only should we see things the way they are—but the way they could be.

"Many people see nothing."

"As long as men dream—there is hope."

"So many of us see clothes, dresses, hairdo's and things.— We never see the person within." If the outside looks well, we presume the inside is too; cars, fancy clothes, big homes, savings accounts, leisure living are not necessarily signs of success.

How can we rest in ease when others hurt so much?— Only if we blind our eyes and close our ears and not feel.

You can never kill a man that dreams.

Great men have great visions.

"Lord, never let us close our minds, become attached to the material, or be satisfied with our own spiritual development. Fill us with Thy will, and may You open our eyes to see the World as You put Your vision in us and then as we know Thy power, we pray Thy will be done on earth as in heaven."

8TH DAY
BIRTH

"Be still, and know that I am God" (Ps. 46: 10).

"Ye must be born again" (John 3: 7).

"Therefore if any man be in Christ he is a new creature: old things are past away; behold all things are become new" (2 Cor. 5: 17).

I see a day of sunshine
            as it
                breaks
            between the clouds.
I see the little seed there
            as it
            pushes past the
                    clods.
I hear an infant crying
            cuddled in its mother's arms—
And that's what—
            Birth's about!
Sunshine and flowers
    Sea Breeze and Waves
a
bird sings its first song—
            of
how sweet is
        Love—
the cry of an infant
    a seed breaks the clod—

A tiny little child
      lifts its voice
            up to God.

a seed is
  born
a cloud is
  made
a friendship is
  begun
a child is
  breathing
a soul is
  reborn.
a man's value is
  re-established
a nation stops to
  breathe new birth.

Oh, I have discovered that birth
      comes from God—

How I love Him:
      With all my soul.

Two lovers
   holding hands—
the music fills the air—
          life
          now is everywhere!
          it's in God's hands.

I saw a child fall on her
          knees to pray

And an old drunk lift up his
                          hands to say—
"God be merciful to me a sinner."

I like to see new grass, a fresh born baby, and a sinner
pray—

We need to pledge allegiance to God—this could be a new
birth for our country.

Have you been born again?

It's Sunday. I think of birth—the day Jesus rose again.
"Wipe away the tears, the guilt, the fears, the problem
years in Jesus' Blood and give me a new Birth."

You have to become a baby—to be born.

Birth is Painful and Bliss.

*"Lord, You know I need a new birth, take away my sin,
greed, and selfishness. Jesus, come into my heart and save
my soul. Fill me now with Your love, peace, and purpose;
create in me a clean heart, in Jesus' name I pray."*

9<small>TH DAY</small>
LOVE

"Beloved, let us love one another; for love is of God" (1 John 4: 7).

"The greatest of these is love" (1 Cor. 13: 13).

"For God is love" (1 John 4: 8).

"For God so loved the world, that he gave his only begotten Son, that whosoever believes in him should not perish but have eternal life" (John 3: 16).

How do you find
        love
Through all the phoney trips—
            egotistical pleasures
                and
            hypocritical words—
How can you find love
        hidden in between
      sensual pleasure, materialism,
                and
           social status

Most "love" is
        a
        way to get what we want.

True love has no value on it
You either love altogether or not at all

True love knows no form of hate.

—Love is active—never passive.

—What greater news than to know
    that God loves me!

—Is love possible?

—There is no chasm that love can't
  bridge.

"So many have lived a lifetime
  searching for love only to find
  phoney substitutes."

"Love makes one go the extra mile,
  turn the other cheek, and give all
  you've got."

"You do not possess love, love possesses
  you."

"Love takes a needy man's hand."

"The Bible is the message of God's
  redeeming love reaching out to man."

I saw
    a mother hold her child—
    a mother bird feed her young
    a couple walking in the grass
                        and
                         I
                        saw
                        Love

Love . . .
    suffereth long
Love . . .
    is kind
Love . . .
    envieth not
Love . . .
    is not puffed up
Love . . .
    is not nasty
Love . . .
    careth for others
Love . . .
    is not angry
Love . . .
    thinketh no evil—
Love . . .
    rejoiceth not in sin
Love . . .
    rejoiceth in truth
Love . . .
    feareth all things
Love . . .
    believeth all things
Love . . .
    hopeth all things
Love endureth all things
    Love never faileth
       (1 Cor. 13: 4–8).

"Love is"—
"Love gives"—

"For I am persuaded, that neither death, nor life, nor angels, nor principalities, nor powers, nor things present, nor things to come, nor height, nor depth, nor any other creature, shall be able to separate us from the love of God, which is in Christ Jesus our Lord" (Rom. 8: 38–9).

"To know Thy Love, O Jesus, is to know true love. As we receive from You may we extend to others. Fill me, overflow me, and use me for ever more."

10TH DAY
TRUTH

"What is truth?" (John 18: 38).

"Jesus said, 'I am the way, the truth, and the life'" (John 14: 6).

'Ye shall know the truth, and the truth shall make you free" (John 8: 32).

Truth
    is the essence
           of fact
the
rape of mind
        the revealing of
valve and
sewer, the loss
      of hypocrisy
      the gain of
      purity
the direction out of confusion
          the hope
          for Peace
it is only in
      truth
that ultimate solution can come;
                For
truth is the filter
        of life
and the
      eternal value,

                    all
            the armies
                        of the world
                        cannot defeat
                            truth
        For
though at times
                    it can be
                    hardly found—
truth makes the
                    weak powerful
    and
        kings tremble—
truth is the world's most
                powerful
                weapon.
truth came . . .
        lived . . .
        died . . .
        rose
            again . . .
And
    shall ultimately prevail.

truth is bigger than
                    any man—
truth prevails
                beyond
    human weakness.
truth is truth
    no matter
                how weak
    the person
            that speaks it.

For many of us the search for truth is too costly, the price too heavy to pay. For others, the truth is too destructive so we never really seek the truth. Content to live the way we are, gripped by fear.

—The first person you have to stop lying to is yourself!

Truth is not for sale.

—The honest eyes of a child saying, "Daddy, I did it," is truth!

To face yourself is heavy.

—How many can stand and face . . . the truth?

—Truth is a priceless commodity.

—Lies brought evil on earth (Gen. 3).

"There is a day of truth coming" . . . Judgment

Truth is not dependent upon man believing it—

—Truth to be *effective* needs to be understood

> If *all* the fronts were
>   ripped away—
>   what would
>   everyone Really
>   See . . .

"Lord, to be true to You, myself, and my fellow man is my great need today. You are truth, Jesus, so fill me with Thyself. Clean me with Your holy blood and love from my hypocrisy and lead me in the truth, in Jesus' name I pray."

11TH DAY
JOY

"The fruit of the Spirit is . . . joy" (Gal. 5: 22).

"O God, thou hast taught me from my youth: and hitherto
have I declared thy wondrous works. Now also when I am
old and grayheaded, O God, forsake me not; until I have
showed thy strength unto this generation, and thy power
to every one that is to come" (Ps. 71: 17–18).

I like to see children play,
                    horses run
                            and
                            eagles
                                    fly.
A lady smile
            and
                grass
                grow.

Jesus came that we might have Life—
                    Real Life—Joy!

Let nothing rob you of joy—

When you think of all you have in Christ—
    that is joy!

I love to watch the moon move slowly across the star-studded
sky, and lie quietly alone in the soft green grass with the
long, thick limbs of an ancient oak hanging overhead. Yes,
I love even to cry and feel tears of cold drip from my

cheek and know that I love and am loved—the soft whisper of words saying "I love you" mixed with the morning dew . . . the feeling of my old home, cows, hogs, chickens and dogs—all making their late evening sound, still fill my ears; Mother's call, "Son, it's supper time," still makes me remember . . . fresh green peas, cornbread, tomatoes, country fried chicken, fresh sweet milk, the whole family around the table—eating together, laughing together, working together—unity—together—like fifty people making sandwiches to feed the hungry—or a prayer meeting before a rally—or a testimony service of spiritual persons, singing in the streets—or riding a jail bus . . . a child lifts up his head to say thanks for his shoes, a lonely widow says, "I'm glad you came by," a doper says, "Jesus set me free." Yes, I love to see a friend wipe away the tears and say, "I feel better now," and for hours I love to read God's Word, make up songs and sing, preach to myself and day-dream, stand before an audience and point the way . . . play with my children, tell stories and roll in the bed, lift up my eyes at close of day and say "Thank you."

"That my lips praise Thee, that my life show Thee, that others see Thee in me and love Thee, in Jesus' name. Amen."

12TH DAY LIFE

"And the Lord God formed man of the dust of the ground, and breathed into his nostrils the breath of life; and man became a living soul" (Gen. 2: 7).

"Jesus said, 'I am come that they might have life, and that they might have it more abundantly' " (John 10: 10).

"And God shall wipe away all tears from their eyes; and there shall be no more death, neither sorrow, nor crying, neither shall there be any more pain: for the former things are passed away" (Rev. 21: 4).

Life is
    living
    giving
    doing
    showing
    going on . . . no matter what.
Life is
    loving
    hurting
    feeling
    needing
    crying
    dying . . . passing on.
Life's a
    trip
    a game
    a shame
    a killing
    a happy feeling—moving on.

Life's a
    baby breathing
    an old man dying
    a lover crying
    a smile upon the face
Life's
    a dream
    a dedication
    a sacrifice
    a reality
Life's
    a battle
    a victory
    a defeat
    a peace
but Life is
    empty without God!

Life is all there is . . .
in spite
    of all that should not be.

—Living is a natural necessity.

"When we see life the way it is—then we can begin to live
the way we should."

—a black life is as important as a white life
—a poor man as important as a rich man
—a whole man as important as a cripple
—a lady as important as a whore
—a child as important as a king
    you as important as me—
                    for what colour is a soul?
                        or
            what life's more value than another?

God deserves our best or nothing.

*"Jesus, You gave Your life for us, may we now give our-
selves to Thee and to our fellow man—make us aware of
all Thy creation, beauty and splendour—as we praise Thy
name. Amen."*

13TH DAY
DEATH

"Death is swallowed up in victory. O death, where is thy
sting? O grave, where is thy victory?" (1 Cor. 15: 54–5).

"Yea, though I walk through the valley of the shadow of
death, I will fear no evil; for thou art with me" (Ps. 23: 4).

"For love is strong as death" (S. of S. 8: 6).

"The living know that they shall die" (Eccles. 9: 5).

Death is an
　　　　open door—
Don't hesitate to walk
　　　　　　　　in—
　　　　　　　　it's the door
to
freedom—
　　　glory's door
　　　　　　Death is Life's
　　　　　　　　　next great adventure
　　　　so step in—
　　　　　　　　without fear.
　　　　Heaven waits . . .
　　　　saints shout . . .
　　　　Jesus calls your name.

to
live—
　　each man must
　　　　　　die

death before death
         is life . . .
             the
     first death
         is as
     important as the second—
                 if you have
             experienced
                 the first
         you need not fear the second.

to
face
death
     is
inevitable
to
fear
death
     is
     to
     fear
         each
     day
to
expect
death
     is
     reality
to
overcome
death
     is
     victory!

to die
    to self
that Jesus may
            fill you
            is
            Life—
        Resting in His Arms
                we
                need not
                        fear—
        when death comes—
                        we
only step from this flesh
        into the fullness
                in that
moment being changed!

Leaves fall from
            trees and
grass dies too—
            green turns to tan—
        birds die—
            and man does too.

Death
    brings us
        face to face
with our true self—
            God . . .
            Judgment! —Heaven, Hell,
                            Eternity!
the man
    not right
        has
            a
        reason to fear dying—

37

Death has a way of equalizing men—

"the urgency of time is death."

"Death has no fear when Jesus is near."

'To be a friend of death, gives a man much freedom."

"A man to be truly powerful must be as willing to die as to live."

"When that moment comes, into Thee my soul shall rest, at Jesus' feet I shall sit. But until then, I give my very best to make the world like Him; in Jesus' name."

14TH DAY
FREEDOM (to be free)

"He is not here; for he is risen, as he said. Come, see the place where the Lord lay" (Matt. 28: 6).

Is there any desire more universal than Freedom?

to walk away from God
                              is not
Freedom—but
            slavery
                              to cast away
the Bible
  for other books
                    is not wisdom
but foolishness—
                    to substitute
God's morality
            for ours—is to
                              exchange
            pearls for trash.
to reject Jesus
            for man's
philosophy—
            is to lose
                  your soul . . .
                  to play the fool—
you see
there is no real freedom
                              except from
                              God

39

God gives freedom from
worry—
sin—
defeat—
lust—
self-centredness—Jesus can set you free.

He
   who is afraid of
   guns—
   threat—
   advice—
     or
       death—
         is not
           free.

Let your mind race—lie back—lift up your hands—feel
the breeze—Be free—let God fill you—open your soul,
speak the name of Jesus. Let every care drift out—let
God's spirit flood you—listen to His Voice—reflect upon
Him. See all he made—love—all its beauty—experience all
of now—every emotion open to feel—to see—to touch—to
smell—to hear—all together—with Him and all He made
—the past gone—the future as a dream—the now reality—
now; wherever you go—or whatever you do—you stay
that way—open—side-stepping disaster—throwing off the
confusing—accepting the necessary—changing the change-
able—never worry—never bound—always loving—ever
giving—little caring of receiving—always praising the name
of Jesus!

Don't let your mind
           be bound
           or your

soul entrapped—

          stay free
          at all cost—

Else everything else

          is lost—
          stay

out of their reach—

          even if they

get to you—

          let them
          find your body—
     pluck out your eyes—

but at all cost—

          Keep your soul
            free.
          as long as your

mind is free

          you are
          never bound!
           go on!
             be free.

"Only the free—live."

"Dare to be free."

"Freedom is always relative"—"Freedom is never free."

"Most people are so bound that when they see a free man —they want to destroy him."

"People cannot understand free people."

When government ceases to offer real freedom it must be changed.

"Thank You for the free spirit You gave us, O Lord, let us not now become entangled with faithless cares but trust in Thy all-suffering, in Christ Jesus our Lord. Amen."

41

15TH DAY
TIME

"In the beginning God created the heaven and the earth" (Gen. 1: 1).

"He hath made everything beautiful in his time" (Eccles. 3: 11).

"Fear not, I am Alpha and Omega, the first and the last" (Rev. 1: 11, 17).

"Surely I come quickly" (Rev. 22: 20).

To everything there is a season
               and
a time to every purpose under the heaven:
                              a time
                                 to
be born
                              a time
to die
                              a time
to plant
                              a time
to pluck up that which is planted:
                              a time
to kill
                              a time
to heal
                              a time
to break down
                              a time

to build up;

a time

to weep

a time

to laugh

a time

to mourn

a time

to dance;

a time

to cast away stones,

a time

to gather stones together;

a time

to embrace,

a time

to refrain from embracing;

a time

to get,

a time

to lose;

a time

to keep,

a time

to cast away;

a time

to rend,

a time

to sew;

a time

to keep silence

a time

to speak;

a time

a time

to love,
                                    a time
to hate;
                                    a time
of war,
                                    a time
of peace;
    (Eccles. 3: 1–8)

        the essence of time is value
        the length of time is experience
        the value of time is priceless
        the use of time is critical
        the condition of time is now
        the waste of time is non-refundable
        time is relative to the experience—

Cast off yesterday's defeats—
        tomorrow's worries and
            live this moment in
                fullness!

*"Dear God, my father, I know that You in Your time sent
Jesus to die for me, now in my time, lead me to live for
Thee, direct me that I waste not a moment, but spend it
in fruitful service in this earth's vineyard in Jesus' name,
Amen."*

16TH DAY
VALUE

"For what shall it profit a man, if he shall gain the whole
world, and lose his own soul?" (Mark 8: 36).

"Beware of covetousness: for a man's life consisteth not
in the abundance of the things which he possesseth" (Luke
12: 15).

Consider that which is of
                         value
evaluate your own
                         energies
reform your life's
                         priorities
devote your energies to
                         these things
detach yourself from the trivial.

never be deceived by size
                         cost
                  time required
                         or
                  public opinion
                         or
                  private opinion
                         or
                  even your own opinion
                         at times.

          "value"?
to build an empire—

45

paint a home—
work on cars—
be a millionaire—
fill a bowl—
         or
     save a soul—
     be a friend—
     feed a brother—
     love an enemy

The seemingly trivial is sometimes the most important.

Remember, everything you do has its return—be careful
what you sow.

"Value is not what you have but who you are! "

"Misplaced values produce misplaced lives."

"You spend your time doing and talking about that which
you consider to be of most value! If this is true, then most
of us are in tragic shape! "

"Great men often do the little things."

"Value is often not understood in materialistic terms."

*"Oh God, open my eyes that I may see the true, discern
that which is of value and commit my life to fulfil the
ultimate purpose, in Jesus' name. Amen."*

17TH DAY
SUCCESS

"Study to show thyself approved unto God, a workman that needeth not to be ashamed, rightly dividing the word of truth" (2 Tim. 2: 15).

"And he shall be like a tree planted by the rivers of water, that bringeth forth his fruit in his season; his leaf also shall not wither; and whatsoever he doeth shall prosper" (Ps. 1: 3).

Success is
helping a child
     to walk,
a friend to smile,
     a hungry man
  to be full
a doper to be free,
     a lonely person
  to know you care
Success is—
  being a man!
     a woman!
for real—
  caring for people—
  knowing how to feel—
Being able to cry
Being willing to die—
dedication without reservation
to the truth—
  at peace with God,
  yourself, and your fellow man,

truthful in living—
happy at heart—
in tune with God
at work in serving your fellow man.

—Success is not what you've got—but what you do with what you have.

—Success is mental attitude.

—Success is doing the will of God.

—Success is living as God created us.

—Success is not success unless it helps others.

"It's tragic that so many live for paper notes of diplomas, degrees, awards, recreation, etc., or for the praise of man, social prestige, influential persons, etc. These are cheap—no matter how costly they are to obtain—success is obeying God—loving Him and knowing Him."

"Our Father which art in heaven, hallowed be Thy name. Thy kingdom come. Thy will be done in earth, as it is in heaven. Give us this day our daily bread. And forgive us our trespasses as we forgive those who trespass against us. And lead us not into temptation, but deliver us from evil. Amen."

This is success!

18TH DAY
FEAR

"Perfect love casteth out fear" (1 John 4: 18).

"They cast him out of the city, and stoned Stephen.
Stephen began calling upon God, and saying 'Lord Jesus,
receive my spirit.' And he kneeled down, and cried with a
loud voice, 'Lord, lay not this sin to their charge.' And
when he had said this, he fell asleep" (Acts 7: 58–60).

Fear to live
    fear
    to
    die—
Fear every day
    everywhere—fear
        got
        to
        keep
            what we have—
we fear—
    loss
      of security—
        fear
        of
        defeat—
        slander—
        reputation—
        and
        ego.
Fear is man's sword
        of suicide

Fear—
    man's constant
           defeat—
Fear—
    respects no one—
           brings
               death to
                  all.
Fear—disrupts
        the
           soul
    shatters—
        peace.
Produces
    anger
    worry
    restlessness
    tension
    sickness
    loneliness
    sadness
    irritability
Fear—
    stifles creativity—
    destroys confidence
    stops initiative
    shatters dreams
Fear—
    destroys love
Fear—
    cannot
        live
          in
        peace

```
      Fear is death
                    even
         before you
                    die

Love—cleans
         fear
         away;
Faith—
      overcomes fear
Compassion—
      ignores fear
Urgency
      never knows fear

Master
      fear
Never
      let it master
                    you.
```

"Fear is more terrible than death—those who fear die a thousand times."

"Lord, I know Thou art real, in You do I trust. With You there is no fear, Thy love casteth it out, so with faith and confidence I live in the midst of fear—never fearful—but fully trusting in Jesus. Amen."

19TH DAY
SAD — HAPPY

"Jesus wept" (John 11: 35).

"Rejoice in the Lord alway" (Phil. 4: 4).

Sad eyes
changed to crystal clear—
guilt and sin gone—in God's
                        great Love—

Jesus' Blood
   makes clean the soul.
gives full freedom
makes us whole—
   no void
      within my
troubled soul
eyes filled with laughter
   joy
   peace
oh the rapture of full release
filled with happiness working
   for peace

      Sad—
         Happy—
            not one
            but two
      Sad—
         Happy—
         that's me!
         you?

Jesus laughed—
  Jesus cried—
Jesus lived—
  Jesus died—
Jesus sad—
  Jesus happy—
Emotion within His breast—

To suffer and be happy; to cry and still rejoice; to care and
still be full; all these and other things all fill the hearts of
Jesus' people.

Sad for suffering humanity—happy for knowing Him.
Weeping with the hurting—at peace within your soul.
Burdened for a needy world—at rest in Jesus. Amen.

Jesus Born
(He had no place to stay) Sad . . . Happy (Saviour came)
Jesus Lived
(He suffered so much) Sad . . . Happy (He showed the
way)
Jesus Died
(He bore so much) Sad . . . Happy (Paid for our sins)
Jesus Rose
(Someone not prepared) Sad . . . Happy (At Jesus' feet)
Jesus is coming again.

*"Lord, though I weep, yet I rejoice; each day the energy,
the time spent helping my fellow men makes me sad—yet
happy. Sometime—if just for a moment, I feel a bit like
you felt so often . . . Amen."*

20TH DAY
JESUS

"My soul doth magnify the Lord" (Luke 1: 46).

Behold a virgin shall bring forth a Son, and thou shall call his name, Jesus. And she brought forth her firstborn son, and wrapped him in swaddling clothes, and laid him in a manger.—And he went down with them and came to Nazareth. And Jesus increased in wisdom and stature, and in favour with God and man. And Jesus said, "Know ye not that I must be about my Father's business?" Jesus, himself began to be about thirty years of age and when he was baptized, went up straightway out of the water; and lo, the heavens were opened unto him and he saw the Spirit of God descending like a dove, and lighting upon him: And lo a voice from heaven saying, "This is my beloved Son, in Whom I am well pleased. And Jesus being full of the Holy Spirit returned from Jordan, and was led by the Spirit into the wilderness, and when he had fasted forty days and forty nights being tempted by Satan he was afterward an hungred. And the angels ministered unto him. And Jesus returned in the power of the Spirit, and from that time Jesus began to preach. He went about all the cities and villages, teaching in their synagogues, and preaching the gospel of the kingdom and healing every sickness and every disease among the people. And Jesus said, "Whosoever will come after me, let him deny himself, and take up his cross and follow me. The foxes have holes and the birds have nests; but the Son of man hath not where to lay his head." (And the hour

being fulfilled, he set his face toward Jerusalem.)
And began to be sorrowful and very heavy and fell
on his face and prayed and his sweat was as it were
great drops of blood falling down to the ground: and
he said, "O my Father, Thy will be done!" Then
they took him away, and all the disciples forsook him
and fled. Pilate saith unto them, "What shall I do
then with Jesus which is called the Christ?" They all
cried, "Let him be crucified." And when they were
come to the place which is called Calvary, there they
crucified him. Then Jesus said, "It is finished," and
he bowed his head and cried, "Father, into Thy
hands I commend my spirit." Then took they the
body of Jesus, and wrapped it in linen and laid it in
a sepulchure that was hewn in stone. Now upon the
first day of the week, very early in the morning, the
angel of the Lord descended from heaven, and came
and rolled back the stone and said, "He is not here;
He is risen!" After these things, Jesus showed himself again to the disciples. Later, he was taken up;
and a cloud received him out of their sight. Behold,
two men in white apparel said, "Why stand ye gazing
up into heaven? This same Jesus which is taken up
from you into heaven shall so come in like manner
as ye have seen him go into heaven."

Matt. 1: 21, 23	Matt. 4: 17	Luke 22: 33
Luke 2: 7	Matt. 9: 35	John 19: 30
Luke 2: 51–2	Mark 8: 34	Luke 23: 46
Luke 2: 49	Matt. 8: 20	John 19: 40
Luke 3: 23	Matt. 26: 37, 39	Luke 23: 53
Matt. 3: 16–17	Luke 22: 24	Luke 24: 1
Luke 4: 1	Matt. 26: 42	Matt. 28: 2, 6
Matt. 4: 2	Luke 22: 54	John 21: 1
Mark 1: 13	Matt. 26: 56	Acts 1: 9 11
Luke 4: 14	Matt. 27: 22	

21ST DAY
PEACE

"Thou wilt keep him in perfect peace, whose mind is stayed on thee" (Isa. 26: 3).

"I will lay me down in peace and sleep" (Ps. 4: 8).

"Seek peace and pursue it" (Ps. 34: 14).

"For he (Jesus) is our peace" (Eph. 2: 14).

"There can be no peace among nations without peace in our own land; no peace in our own land until peace is a reality in the home; the home will never have peace until each person there has peace in his own heart—there is no peace within, until there is peace with God."

—The problem is not so much world peace—as personal peace.

—Any solution for peace that ignores the individual need is doomed to failure!

—The problem is not laws but men; change the heart and you change the world.

—One prayer meeting is worth a thousand peace conferences.

—Men who are not filled with peace cannot create peace.

—Peace cannot be forced—or enforced.

—"I've noticed—many advocators of 'peace' have little peace within."

—"Don't hit me with your Peace Sign! "

—The only peace some have is when they are at war!

> Armies cannot establish peace.
> Money cannot buy it.
> Laws cannot create it.
> Only God can provide it.
> > Ignore Him, and
> you can never find it!

"Peace to most is an elusive dream."

"Peace is the life's quest of many—the possession of few."

"Peace is a gift—yet only from God."

I'd rather meet a "peace" man
> > than a "war" man.
I'd rather have a "flower child"
> > than a "hate" child.
I'd rather teach my child
> to love
> than to kill.
I'd rather teach him how
> > to share—
> than be rich.
I'd rather teach him how
> > to pray—
Be fair,
Truthful
> and know the Lord
> than anything.

Government can hardly afford peace—the economics of war is too great! Often times government thrives on fear and suspicion, it keeps the people together hating the same thing, and working for a common goal. Hitler said, "Give the people something to hate." This still is a common, though hidden tactic.

Jesus spans the gulf of sin, and gives us perfect peace with God.

"Jesus is the only door to real peace."

"The way of peace, O Lord, is Thy way. As we live in a world that follows not Thy way, may I remain at peace with Thee and with my fellow man through Jesus' blood. Amen."

22ND DAY QUIET TIME

"Be still, and know that I am God" (Ps. 46: 10).

    Quiet time—
      moments alone with
  myself
    and
        God—
  time to be open—
    free—
      clear and
        listening
  to Jesus speak—
    open to
  the fullness of His Spirit
  a time of refreshment and
    cleansing—
      quiet time—
  moments with the master
  too pure to
    transfer—
  too holy to
    speak of
  fulfilling all needs—
  giving strength to meet
    every crisis—
  quiet time—
    a priceless moment.

So often we find Jesus going off alone to pray, to think, to fellowship with the Father. Before most major events in

His life he was alone in prayer. He never tried to rush those moments. They were most valuable to Him. Study the lives of Abraham, Joshua, Moses, Elisha, David, the prophets, John the Baptist, Paul, to name a few, and you see the quiet times of spiritual renewal that were the key to their public minutes.

Quiet time is not to be compared to wasted time, it is to be a time of inward search, heavenly revelation, and spiritual power. It should be the basis of victory in our daily lives and in witnessing. Elijah heard the still small voice of God speaking after he had tried to hear God in the storm, lightning, thunder. Maybe you should stop and be still long enough to hear "God's still small voice" speaking to you.

Quiet times are times of power—
Never get too busy to take time to pray and be alone with God.
Be still, quiet, and know God, then herald the truth across the land.

"Dear Jesus, You are with me each moment; that I know. But those times that I spend alone with You Lord are so precious to me; when You and I, O Father, run down to the beach, play in the clover, and visit quietly in your mountains or kneel at your altar; Thank You, O God, for Thy lasting presence."

23RD DAY
LIVING IN VICTORY

Men ought always to pray and not to faint, for you are of God, little children, and have overcome them because greater is he that is in you, than he that is in the world. The Lord knoweth how to deliver the godly out of temptation for there hath no temptation taken you but such as is common to man: but God is faithful, who will not suffer you to be tempted above that you are able, but will with the temptation also make a way of escape that you may be able to bear it. For it is God which worketh in you both to will and to do his good pleasure. This I say then, walk in the Spirit and ye shall not fulfil the lust of the flesh. The fruit of the Spirit is love, joy, peace, longsuffering, gentleness, goodness, faith, meekness, and self-control. They that are Christ's have crucified the flesh with the affections and lusts.

But my God shall supply all your need according to his riches in glory by Christ Jesus. Therefore, I can do all things through Christ which strengtheneth me.

Have no anxiety over anything; but in everything by prayer and supplication with thanksgiving let your requests be made known unto God. And be not drunk with wine, wherein is excess; but be filled with the Spirit; speaking to yourselves, to one another, in psalms and hymns and spiritual songs, singing and making melody in your heart to the Lord; giving thanks always for all things unto God. And the peace of God, which passeth all understanding, shall keep your hearts and minds through Christ Jesus. Finally, brethren, whatsoever things are true, honest, just, pure, lovely, of good report; if there be any virtue, and any praise, think on these things. For I have learned in whatsoever state I am, therewith to be content. Finally, my brethren, rejoice evermore, pray without ceasing, in everything give thanks, preach the word, abstain from all appearance of evil, quench not the spirit, establish your hearts, for the coming of the Lord draweth near.

Luke 18: 1
1 John 4: 4
2 Pet. 2: 9
1 Cor. 10: 13
Phil. 2: 13
Gal. 5: 16
Gal. 5: 22–4
Phil. 4: 19

Phil: 4: 13
Phil. 4: 6
Eph. 5: 18–20
Phil. 4: 7–8, 11
2 Thess. 3: 1
1 Thess. 5: 16–19, 22
2 Tim. 4: 2
Jas. 5: 8

24TH DAY
REVOLUTION

"Therefore if any man be in Christ, he is a new creation—
old things are passed away; behold all things are become
new" (2 Cor. 5: 17).

One stepped down one day
to show the way for a better day.

Hear the sounds of
hate, guns, blood,
Oh, hear the sound of
cries, fears, lawlessness, destruction.
Hear the sounds of
Revolution . . .
Listen again to—
the sound of love—
God's Love—
reaching out—
caring—helping—
making new—
Jesus Christ—
Revolution of the Soul!
to lift up Jesus Christ—to
see Him
know Him and
love Him
And to accept Him
as Lord—
is heavy—
it's Revolution—for real.

Jesus said "go"
     to the streets—
          homes—
          shops
          businesses
          schools
          universities
          prisons
          radio
          TV
          books—
               everywhere to
               everyone—
                    all the time!

—Stand firm in the midst of the most deadly assault; stand by the cross of the King.

—A changed heart makes a changed man.

—A good revival is better than a million laws.

When man gets right with God and loves God with all his heart he then loves his neighbours as himself. Christ within us leads us to a right relationship with our fellow man, meaning that we are actively concerned with injustice, hate, hunger, physical as well as spiritual problems. This is revolution, the Revolution we need; Christ changing you and the world around you—a light in darkness—the way of hope in a sea of despair.

"Oh, Jesus, may we truly be in Your revolution, lead us to set the example and show the way to true and good change in our hearts and world, for Thy glory. Amen."

25TH DAY
THE BIBLE

"All scripture is given by inspiration of God, an
profitable for doctrine, for reproof, for correction,
instruction in righteousness" (2 Tim. 3: 16).

As man gropes in darkness
  Looking for the day
The Bible is
  Light—
to show the way,
Truth to speak on the
  issues of today,
Enlightenment for tomorrow—
  strength for
    today!
from its pages
  flow the love
from its paper
  uncontaminated truth
you see—Christ,
  portrayed, living Lord, to
save,
make whole,
  remould. Hold—
the Book—
  God's pure word,
fill your heart
  with water . . .
    from the quenching well.

Hand me the Bible,
        I'd
Like to read for a while—
and
Live in the pages of
        truth . . .
                for a moment.

"I believe."

Fools pit themselves against God's Word—
        they pass—but
                not His Word!

—The unsettled life is not fully settled in the Word.

—The Bible is clear truth—the problem comes in man's rationalization.

—Give me one book—if only one—the Bible.

"Our Father, lead us to understand Thy truth, live it and follow in Your Holy Will. May foolish men not cast shadows of darkness over Your Word's Holy Light and may we see clearly Thy face in Your Word! Amen."

26^{TH DAY}
HATE

"Whosoever hateth his brother is a murderer" (1 John 3: 15).

"If a man say, I love God, and hateth his brother, he is a liar" (1 John 4: 20).

Hate,
  the ugly face
        of
        death
        bitterness
          fear—
the
curse of wickedness—
            hell's
        open door.
Hate,
  Heaven's enemy
  Satan's friend
Hate,
the end of reason
           the
pollution of mind
           the
tomb of civilization.

to go the other
  mile
turn the
  other cheek—

to give cool water
   to your enemy
     to
give and
  give and
give and give
        and
love and
  love
to even smile
  and
laugh
      and keep your
head up
and your heart full
no matter what you face—
  to
look up and
     Love—
even the hateful—
  the hating—
overcome . . . Hate
  by Love—

"Jesus, it looks like we passed You by—put something in our hearts beside You and your Love, what a bummer the world is without You as Lord. Yes Jesus, start with me, clean my heart from hate—make me to Love as You. Amen."

27TH DAY INJUSTICE

"Defend the poor and fatherless: do justice to the afflicted and needy" (Ps. 82: 3).

"But let judgment run down as waters, and righteousness as a mighty stream" (Amos 5: 24).

—Government must be just—

—to be silent—in the face of injustice and adversity—is to be greatly deceived.

—The Bible message is filled with—justice—truth—virtue—

to put materialism ahead of human value is injustice!

—The personal value of one man is not expendable.

—When our value system centres in:

material
things—
name—
possession—
power—
achievement—

Rather than equal spirit value—
injustice is unavailable!

Jesus spoke the truth—He offended—He died
He mended—He arose
He still speaks
truth
Do you?

to be silent against injustice—is anything worse?

to
refuse to speak—
            to sleep—
while others suffer—
                die—
I'll make my bed
            with the
Just—
    even if it means
death—
For he who will not oppose
                evil is
dead—already—
the suffering
need a friend—
may I
    never fail.

"Unto Thee, our Lord, we lift our voices, hear our prayer, and may Thy will be done on earth as in heaven, then we know injustice, prejudice and suppression shall be erased from the mind of man. Show Thy way through us to others so blind they will not see or hear Thy voice. Lift the oppressed and may I stand for Thy justice on earth. Amen."

28TH DAY
KINDNESS

"Be kindly affectioned one to another with brotherly love"
(Rom. 12: 10).

to give the beggar
more than a dime
but
a little time
is kindness;
  to lend a hand
to
a fallen friend
  is kindness;
to say "hello"
  to the
stranger
at the door—
  to let
him in
  is kindness;
to stand with a man
  when he's at his end—
to be his friend—
  is kindness;
to feed the poor—
to open a door,
clothe the naked
send a card—
    a smile—
to get involved
  is kindness.

to not demand—
  but be willing to give
to live
  in peace,
to love all men—
to help
  a child
feed a
  hungry man
mend the wing
  of a
fallen bird or
speak a word,
to live a life in peace
with our fellow man
  is kindness!

—Kindness is the refinement of life.

—Kindness is not weakness but strength.

—Kindness is more powerful than the sword.

    Kindness lets you know the
      heart's in
        tune . . .

*"Lord, Thy kindness to us is clearly shown, now grant us
the strength and fullness of Thy Spirit that we may show
to others, as You have shown to us, the perfect example
of love, self-control, and kindness."*

29TH DAY
MARRIAGE

"So God created man in his own image, in the image of God created he him; male and female created he them. And God blessed them . . . and said be fruitful and multiply . . . and God saw everything that he made, and, behold, it was very good" (Gen. 1: 27, 28, 31).

Marriage—
> man
> woman

Marriage—
> love
> beauty

Marriage—
> sex
> union

Marriage—
> life
> birth

Marriage—
> children
> knowledge

Marriage—
> learning
> sharing

Marriage—
> sickness
> health

Marriage—
> needs
> wealth

Marriage—
        ageing
        experiencing
Marriage—
        tears
        joy
Marriage—
        companionship
        caring
Marriage—
        prayer
        death
Marriage—
        blessed
        of God.

—Marriage without God is not even half complete.

—the home—more significant than all laws in determining what kind of world this will be.

—marriage is not for convenience but for a lifetime.

"Lord, You have let the two of us share more than words could ever express, the tears, joys and life that has been ours is so priceless You've blessed our home. Four little bundles of life and beauty You have given to us. Grant Thy grace that our house is a place You love to visit and stay. Amen."

30TH DAY
TEMPTATION

"God will allow no temptation to be insurmountable but
will with the temptation show you how to escape so that
you will not be overcome" (1 Cor. 10: 13).

"The Lord knoweth how to deliver the godly out of
temptations" (2 Pet. 2: 9).

—Strength is
              produced in
testing.

—When you resist
              and
              overcome
you
are ready for another step.

—it's only in testing
              that
true power is
              revealed.

—Temptation is
              a laboratory
of self-analysis

—Temptation is not a
              once
and for all victory

—To fill one's mind with the right is the best way to overcome the wrong.

—To be wise to Satan
            to know his plan of
            attack is
                wisdom.

Temptation is ever present but not all powerful—Jesus is Lord!

Having received Him, He dwelleth within—all things are under His feet, King of kings and Lord of lords. We can now as a Christian accept the throne possession of Christ. His Spirit within, He leads. Having overcome Satan and being creator, His power is sufficient. Therefore, we can have full confidence in His sufficiency.

"Lord, it is a joy to walk in Thy power—to know You, and know that in You all my sufficiency lies. Fill me with Your Spirit and lead me with Your gentle hand. Amen."

31ST DAY
BROTHERHOOD

"God is no respecter of persons" (Acts 10: 34).

"Love one another" (Rom. 13: 8).

to treat
   all men as brothers
to love,
respect,
and
give,
regardless of
   social status
   colour
   economics
   customs
      or
   styles—
to care no matter what the condition,
to give no matter what the attitude,
to love without regard of return,
to let God live through us,
               this
               is
brotherhood in its truest form!

—When we cease to be brothers, we cease to be men!

—Real brotherhood makes an "out of sight" neighbour-
hood!

Brotherhood is
        loving,
caring
and
getting . . .
        involved!

Brotherhood is
        caring for others
        as you care
        for
        yourself.

Brotherhood is the basis
        of
        a
        just
        society.
True brotherhood would—Revolutionize
        our
        society and
        lives.

"Lord as You have loved us, acted and got involved, may we in Thy example, follow in Your steps. May this prayer not be empty words, but fruitful in my daily life as You care for others through me!"

32ND DAY
TODAY

"Today if you will hear his voice, harden not your hearts"
(Heb. 3: 15).

"Whereas you know not what shall be on the morrow"
(Jas. 4: 14).

Today is all the time I have
the past
   is
yesterday, tomorrow's dawn may never come,
I live today—
learning from yesterday, dreaming of tomorrow
yet alive now—my love, my care, my life
must be lived today, not yesterday or tomorrow
but now—now is the time to
        pray—
         to
        play—
         and
        to be
now is the moment of love—
            peace—
            beauty—
            joy—
this is the time to care—
        to bare—
        to decide—
        to
           win the victory . . .

today—
this moment is all I have—
my
best is all that's worthy—
God wants it—
          the
World needs it—
               I
               can do no less.
Yes—
today—will be my fullest
                    day—
the best day I've ever lived—
in God's will
          He leads me—
loves me—
          and fills me—
to
make
     this day my best is
     His
dream.
today—better than yesterday,
                    today—
My day to live to the fullest.

*"May I not fail today to be all I could, natural, resting in
Thee, creating, alert, loving. Awake to every emotion,
beauty, and need, filled with Thy Presence, hearing Thy
voice at day's end saying, well done."*

33^{RD DAY} SELF CONTROL

"The fruit of the Spirit is—self control" (Gal. 5: 22–3).

—full freedom in living is found in resting in the Lord.

to do what
  should
    be
done,
to refrain from
       that
       which
should not—
       is
       control.
to master your
       tongue
so that you will say the best
       things—
to master your heart
      so you want
        whatever is best
to master your attitudes,
          motives,
          emotion,
so
that
you can
  reach the highest level
                 of
completion and fulfilment!

—When your heart is filled with the Holy Spirit of God, then God-like reflections become the natural way of your living.

—whatever the crisis—stay in control.

—to be master of your emotions, actions, reactions, and mind is power!

—change is always easier from the inside out, than from the outside in.

—we in Christ are to be masters of ourselves, not having our passions, emotions, and desires master us.

"Lord, today, in this moment I rest in Thee, I look at Jesus. Make me I pray, like Him, for in Him I can be wise in my speaking, alert in my thinking, considerate in my actions, and compassionate in my heart."

34TH DAY
FORGIVENESS

"The blood of Jesus Christ, his Son, cleanseth us from all sin. If we confess our sins, he is faithful and just to forgive us our sins and to cleanse us from all unrighteousness." (1 John 1: 7, 9).

to be clean—
to
at
long last,
   rest
with a new heart,
guilt
   gone . . .
heart full,
Purpose—future lies ahead,
defeat—
behind—
God filling your heart—
eyes
clear—Shame erased with
               Love—
God's
grace revealed—
emptiness—filled—
Love controlling!

to
forgive others,
     as
God

forgives us,
to
know a life—free from

> hate
> resentment
> jealousy

and vengeance—
  to love others—
    forgive them
as we want God to forgive us,
to
be bigger than self defeating

> attitudes—
> to
> be

  as big as
        forgiveness!

—forgiveness sounds too good to be true!

—in forgiveness there is freedom!

—to forgive someone does you more good than them!

"Father, it's so easy for us to resent others, and keep the grudges and evil attitudes in our hearts, but with You in us we just can't stay that way. Forgive us as we forgive our brothers; may we see that we are the most guilty of all."

35TH DAY
FAITH

"Lord, I believe" (Mark 9: 24).

"The just shall live by faith" (Rom. 1: 17).

"Your faith should not stand in the wisdom of men, but in the power of God" (1 Cor. 2: 5).

Faith is
  believing
    the Spirit impulse
      from God!
Faith—
  not to fear
But
to believe—
Faith—not in
      elusive dreams
but
in God—
in
Faith receiving Jesus—
Faith in
His divine Will—
walking in faith!
walking with God.
Faith . . .
Knowing Him—
Hearing His Voice—
following His call

Faith—
  to go on—
    whatever the Hell.
Faith
  so strong you can never
            be
  deterred, defeated, or discouraged.
Faith
overcoming all enemies—
going on! Looking up!

—Faith is being open to God—to hear Him and do His will.

—Faith is trust!

—Faith is the stability of life—it is the anchor in a troubled sea.

—You either believe, or you don't.

—God is with me, I walk in faith, what have I to fear!

—Faith dreams—then makes it reality!

—"Living Faith"

—Faith that is not relative to everyday life—is not real faith.

"Lord, I believe You, I know You—I love You. My Jesus, what life You give, with all my soul I cry, 'Lord, I believe!' "

36TH DAY
WORDS

"Let the words of my mouth, and the meditations of my
heart, be acceptable in thy sight, O Lord, my strength and
my redeemer" (Ps. 19: 14).

Some people say, "oh, I didn't mean that, it just came
out"—but I believe we really mean all we say—we just
hate to face it.

Words; an expression of
                         truth or lies,
Love or
deceit,
  virtue or
  vileness
words—creative beauty or
                     soul corruption.
Words can either build or
               destroy,
bind or
  tear down—
create peace or
  produce Hell
Words are powerful
like an atom
or empty—
  false—and
    fraud.
Words can be
con-games;
echo chambers, and

cover ups—
   or
Words can be
  real,
expression of true sincerity,
              love and
                  honesty,
but
the latter words
are
truly
  hard to
    find!

—How many people today will hear someone say, "I love you"—oh, but few will be for real.

—a lot of words—a little action.

—some people's words aren't worth the effort of talking.

—it's not what you say—"it's really who you are! "

—behind my words—who am I?

"Jesus, make my words true like You, words that from my heart proceed in love and honesty—words not to cut or condemn, but to share the love of You with, not phony, but real in Thy truth. Amen."

37TH DAY HURT

"Jesus wept" (John 11: 35).

"When He saw the multitudes He was moved with compassion" (Matt. 9: 36).

Sure I've hurt—
haven't
        you—but
it means you can still feel
not
cold like steel,
but
real—alive—sensitive—
human—
hurting—
   suffering with others—
   weeping with them—
for
loving is hurting—
                in this
                    world.
don't fear to
            hurt—
fear when you don't.
The
greatest lover of all time—
                        hurt
the most—
        He
did the most—

so
thank God you can still feel—
tears—
compassion—
pain—
sorrows—
   through this you experience
faith—
achievement—
maturity—
strength—
wisdom—
love—
   so
   Hurt—
When men suffer—
   cry
   hunger
   despair
   search—
    Hurt—
enough to give your life
                 not in
                    complaints
but in Love, Action, and Faith.

"Thank You, Lord, that You became flesh, and know all the human desires, and hurt like us, yet overcame all evil and won the final victory. Heal our sin-caused hurt, but make our seared hearts open to Thy true love and our brother's needs. Make us to care as You, and give our lives in the beauty of ministry in Thy name."

38TH DAY
HOPE

"Fear not, O land; be glad and rejoice: for the Lord will do great things" (Joel 2: 21).

"And I saw a new heaven and a new earth" (Rev. 21: 1).

if you look real close,
you
can see
the sunshine
breaking through
yonder
cloud.
Sh—
Be very quiet—Sh—
I
hear a new song
in the Sky—
getting closer—
closer—

I saw one turn the other cheek—
a
beggar fed—
a sinner saved.
I saw
hope—
for a better day—

Hope!
you lazy bones,
get
up—get it on!

There is hope!

—God so loved the world that he gave his only begotten Son that whosoever believeth in him should not perish but have everlasting life (John 3: 16).

—If we confess our sin He will cleanse us.

—If any man be in Christ he is a new creature—trust Him now.

"Lord, I believe, forgive my sins, come into my heart, I give my life to God. Thank You. I know You'll never leave me—I love You Lord, in Jesus' name. Amen."

"Lord, in Thee there is the strength for a better day, a new world in Your image. For the guilty, the sad, the lonely, the confused, the needy, lead us to show them the hope of a new birth, the hope of a way out of darkness, and the hope of strength to go on the way. In Jesus' name. Amen."

39TH DAY
GOVERNMENT

"The government shall be upon his shoulder" (Isa. 9: 6).

the human ill
            lies in the heart . . .
no law can change
            this land.
it's the way a man
                really feels
that makes him live the way he does;
            that makes him hate, and
            lie and kill;
it's
not the invention
            of the wheel
            or
            gaming clubs or dirty shows,
it's in the heart . . .
                yea in the soul—
an
emptiness deep within;
the action of the outer life
only reveals that
            even
            worse things lie within;
no programme here can change
                the man, not a pill,
            a drink
            a chick
            a dollar bill;

a law, a troop, or a revolution . . . only Jesus,
the soul solution for
                    sin pollution! . . .

The greatest defenders of justice, mercy, and righteousness
were the Old Testament prophets and lawgivers. Their
voices and action cut as sharp knives flashing—against
national leaders, oppressors, and evil—their prophetic
voices and trail of blood led to Jesus who made the
standards even higher; the New Testament men like John
the Baptist, Peter, and Paul attacked evil and died with
their voices lifting high the truth; the long fight against
suppression and evil permissiveness is not a once-for-all
victory; but each generation must rise up and light up
God's holy way for men to live. The leaders of government
are to be the servants of the people, not the imposing
masters, they must be open, spirit-filled, and devout men
of God, for us to accept any other standard is to destroy
the message of God to the nations in the Old and New
Testaments. We must as today's prophets preach the same
message, and even, if we must, pay the same price.

*"O Lord, lead us that we may choose leaders among us
who are Your men, that through them You may dispense
Your love, mercy, justice, and righteousness. Forgive us
for expecting so little of Thee, O God, bless our nation and
every other nation and all our brothers and sisters
wherever they may be, in Jesus' name, Amen."*

40TH DAY
SELFISHNESS

"Brethren . . . by love serve one another" (Gal. 5: 13).

"Love . . . is not selfish" (1 Cor. 13: 5).

Each on his own trip—
getting what he can
speaking words
    of
        self-denial
            yet . . .
Self . . . is supreme!
the idol of
    self-interest
        is Lord.
Hear the same voice saying
"Jesus, I love you! "
To put myself
    in the lowest place
to serve the unknown—
    to live and give
without applause,
    to walk in humility;
even in honour, not egotistical;
in success,
        not haughty;
in failure,
            not vengeful;
not demanding of others . . . but
            considerate, and
            understanding of human weakness;

Ready to aid our fellow man;
Ready to reach out . . . and
                          never

turn
   in
   bitterness against that person!

Selfishness . . .
   the extreme tragedy of human weakness,
the tyrant of
          passion
the defeat of higher
               ideas
the suppression of freedom
the limit of love . . .
                the
                basis of evil!
—the selfish man is the cancer of society.—

—the selfish are never satisfied.—
—the selfish can serve—but never in humility.—

"O God, free me from the passions of my own flesh, selfish will and self-seeking attention. Fill me with Thy Holy Spirit that each impulse I feel shall be heavenly inspired and that I seek the best in Thy will, toward myself and my fellow man, in Jesus' name. Amen."